FRANCES BRIGGS

PHOTOGRAPHY BY

FRANCES JANISCH,
PETER BAASCH, &
DARON CHATZ

LAUREL
GLEN

RAW

First published in the United States by
Laurel Glen Publishing
5880 Oberlin Drive, San Diego, CA 92121-4794
www.advantagebooksonline.com
Copyright © in text: Frances Briggs 2000
Copyright © in photographs, as on this page, right
Copyright © in published edition: Struik Publishers
(Pty) Ltd 2000

All notations of errors or omissions should be
addressed to Laurel Glen Publishing, editorial
department, at the above address. All other
correspondence (author inquiries, permissions and
rights) concerning the content of this book should
be addressed to New Holland Ltd, Garfield House,
86-88 Edgware Rd., London W2 2EA.

Library of Congress Cataloging-in-Publication Data

Briggs, Frances.
    Raw : design by nature / Frances Briggs ;
photography by Frances Janisch, Peter Baasch &
Daron Chatz.
        p. cm.
    ISBN 1-57145-572-8
    1. Interior decoration. 2. Interior architecture.
I. Janisch, Frances. II. Baasch, Peter. III. Chatz, Daron.

NK2110 .B74 2001
747--DC21
                                    2001035308

Designer: Petal Palmer
Publishing manager: Linda de Villiers
Editor: Gail Jennings
Proofreader: Brenda Brickman

1 2 3 4   04 03 02 01

Reproduction by Hirt & Carter Cape (Pty) Ltd
Printed and bound by Craft Print (Pte) Ltd,
Singapore

PHOTOGRAPHIC CREDITS

A = Architect © = Copyright L = Location

Listed in order: Photographer, Stylist and
Architect/Copyright holder/Location
Photographers: FJ = Frances Janisch, DC = Daron
Chatz FB = Frances Briggs, PB = Peter Baasch,
CF = Craig Fraser
Architects: JS = Johann Slee, SR = Sylvio Rech,
PL = Pierre Lombart, KO = Kate Otten,
CG = Charl Groenewald

Stylists: FB = Frances Briggs, LJ = Laura Jamieson
COC = Cathy O'Cleary, LF = Lynn Fraser
NVW = Natalie van Wyk, KN = Kassie Naidoo
Locations: LOTB = The Lodge on the Bay,
SAP = St. Augustine's Priory, T = Timbuktu
Copyright holders ELLE Decoration = *Elle
Decoration* Magazine, ELLE = *Elle Magazine*,
SLV = St Leger & Viney

Cover, from left: FJ/FB/JS(A); FJ/COC/ELLE
Decoration©; DC/FB/PL(A); PB/ELLE©; page 2:
FJ/FB/JS(A); page 6, clockwise from top left:
DC/LJ/LOTB(L); DC/FB/PL(A); PB/FB/SR(A);
FJ/COC/ELLE Decoration©; FJ/SAP(L);
DC/LJ/LOTB(L); DC/LJ/LOTB(L); FJ/LJ/ELLE
Decoration©; PB/COC/ELLE Decoration©; page
10: DC/FB/PL(A); page 13: DC/FB/PL(A); page 14:
DC/FB/PL(A); page 15 left and right: DC/FB/PL(A);
pages 16-7: FJ/FB/JS(A); page 18: DC/FB/PL(A); page
19: DC/LJ/ELLE Decoration©; page 20: DC/LJ/ELLE
Decoration©; page 21: PB/COC/ELLE
Decoration©; page 22: FJ/SAP(L); page 22: CF/ELLE
Decoration©; page 24 left: PB/FB/SR(A); page 24
right: DC/FB; page 25: FJ/KO(A); page 26: FJ/SAP(L);
page 27: FJ/SAP(L); Page 28: DC/FB/PL(A); page 31:
FJ/LJ/ELLE Decoration©; page 32: PB/COC/ELLE
Decoration©; page 33: PB/COC/ELLE
Decoration©; page 34: DC/FB/PL(A); page 35:
DC/FB/PL(A); page 36 left and right: PB/COC/ELLE
Decoration©; page 37 right: FB (stylist and
photographer); pages 38-9: DC/FB/JS(A); page 40:
DC/LJ/LOTB(L); page 41, clockwise from top left:
FJ/FB; DC/FB; FJ/FB; page 42: FJ/FB/JS(A); page 43:
DC/LJ/ELLE Decoration©; page 44 left and right:
DC/FB/PL(A); page 45: DC/FB/PL(A); pages 46-7:
DC/FB/JS(A); page 48, clockwise from top left: FB
(stylist and photographer); FB (stylist and
photographer); FJ; DC/FB; DC/LOTB(L); DC; DC;
PB; DC/LJ/ELLE Decoration©; page 50: FJ/FB/JS(A);
page 53: PB/COC/ELLE Decoration©; page 54 left:
PB/COC/ELLE DECORATION©; page 54 right:
DB/COC/ELLE DECORATION©; page 55:
FJ/COC/ELLE Decoration©; pages 56-7: FJ/FB/JS(A);
page 58: FJ/COC/ELLE Decoration©; page 59:
PB/COC/KO(A); page 60-1: FJ/COC/ELLE
Decoration©; page 61 right: FJ/COC/ELLE
Decoration©; page 62 FJ/FB/JS(A); page 63
PB/COC/ELLE Decoration©/KO(A); page 64
top and below: DC/COC/CG(A); page 65:
DC/COC/CG(A); page 66: FJ/COC/ELLE
Decoration©; page 67 top: PB/COC/ELLE
Decoration©; page 67 below: DC/FB/JS(A);
page 68: PB/FB/SR(A); page 69: DC/COC/CG(A);
page 70: DC/ELLE Decoration©; page 73:
PB/COC/ELLE Decoration©; page 74-5:
DC/FB/PL(A); page 75: PB/COC/ELLE
Decoration©; page 76 clockwise from top left:
PB/COC/ELLE Decoration©; DC/LJ/LOTB(L); FJ/FB;
PB/COC/ELLE Decoration©; page 77:
DC/LJ/LOTB(L); page 78: FJ/LJ/ELLE Decoration©;
page 79 top: FJ/LJ/ELLE Decoration©; page 79

below: FB (photographer); page 80 left: DC/LJ/ELLE
Decoration©; page 80 right: DC/LJ/LOTB(L); page
81 left: DC/LJ/LOTB(L); page 81 right: DC/LJ/ELLE
DECORATION©; page 82: FJ/COC/ELLE
Decoration©; page 85: PB/COC/ELLE
DECORATION©; page 86 left: PB/COC/ELLE
Decoration©; page 86 right: DC/LJ/ELLE
Decoration©; page 87: FJ/COC/ELLE
DECORATION©; page 87 right: PB/KN/ELLE©;
pages 88-89: FJ/ELLE Decoration©; page 90:
PB/FB/SR(A); page 91: PB/COC/ELLE Decoration©;
page 92: PB/KN/ELLE©; page 93: PB/COC/ELLE
Decoration©; page 94: PB/FB/SR(A); page 95:
FJ/FB/JS(A); page 96 top and below: FJ/FB; page 97:
PB/FB/SR(A); pages 98-99: FJ; page 100: DC/FB;
page 101: DC/FB; page 102: PB/ELLE©; page 105:
PB/COC/T(L); page 106: DC/COC/SLV©; page 107
top, centre and below: DC/COC/SLV©; page 108
left and right: DC/COC/SLV©; page 109:
DC/COC/SLV©; pages 110-11: FJ/COC/ELLE
Decoration©; page 110 right: PB/COC/ELLE
Decoration©; page 112 clockwise from top left:
DC/LJ/LOTB(L); DC/COC/ELLE Decoration©;
DC/COC/ELLE Decoration©; DC/COC/ELLE
Decoration©; DC/LJ/ELLE Decoration©;
DC/LJ/LOTB(L); DC/LJ/LOTB(L);
pages 114-15: PB/LJ/ELLE Decoration©; page 116:
DC/LJ/ELLE Decoration©; DC/LJ/LOTB(L); page
118: FJ/FB; page 119: FJ/FB/JS(A); Page 120:
FJ/COC/ELLE Decoration©; page 121 top:
PB/COC/ELLE©; page 121 below: PB/NVW/ELLE
Decoration©; page 122: FJ/COC/ELLE
Decoration©; page 125: DC/LF/ELLE Decoration©;
page 126 left: FJ/COC/ELLE Decoration©; page
126 right PB/COC/ELLE Decoration©; page 127
left and right: PB/COC/ELLE©; page 128:
DC/LJ/LOTB(L); page 129: DC/LJ/ELLE
Decoration©; page 130: DC/LJ/ELLE Decoration©;
page 131: PB/LJ/ELLE Decoration©; page 132:
DC/LJ/ELLE Decoration©; page 133: DC/FB/JS(A);
page 134, clockwise from top left: PB/COC/ELLE
Decoration©; DC/LJ/ELLE Decoration©; PB/LJ/ELLE
Decoration©; DC/COC/ELLE Decoration©;
PB/COC/ELLE Decoration©; DC/LJ/ELLE
Decoration©; DC/FB; PB/COC/ELLE Decoration©;
DC/LJ/ELLE Decoration©; page 136 top and
below: FB (stylist and photographer; page 137:
FJ/FB; page 138: DC/LJ/ELLE ELLE Decoration©;
page 139: DC/LJ/ELLE Decoration©; page 140 top
and below right: FJ/COC/ELLE Decoration©; page
140 below left: DC/LJ/ELLE Decoration©; page
141: FJ/COC/ELLE Decoration©

AUTHOR'S ACKNOWLEDGMENTS

Heartfelt thanks to Uschi and Peter Stuart, Rita and
Chris Blignaut, Mavis Briggs, Leana Swanepoel,
Frances, Daron, Peter, Cathy, all the architects and
the team at Struik for their generous help in
making this book happen.

RAW

RAW

RAW

METAL
10

WOOD
28

PLASTER
50

MASONRY
70

CERAMIC
82

TEXTILES
102

FIBER
122

SUPPLIERS
142

RAW

RAW

INTRODUCTION

In a world that is increasingly demanding, there is no better "rescue remedy" than to connect with nature. Feeling the earth beneath our bare feet or lying on a patch of grass and staring at the clouds overhead is pure bliss. These simple pleasures keep us in touch with the rhythms of our natural environment, and on a deep level, they nurture and nourish our souls.

Before the rapid urbanization of the past few centuries, people would build their homes using raw materials gleaned from the earth and vegetation around them. They lived close to the natural world and used natural materials, imbued with "good vibrations."

Today we yearn for these vibrations to ground us and offer a calm center within the whirlwind.

Unfortunately much of this building knowledge has been lost to us. We no longer sleep and live in circular structures close to the ground as our ancestors did. Our homes are raised above the ground or separated by concrete foundations, with no connection to the earth. We are surrounded by artificial light and plastic surfaces. It is this separation from nature that leaves us feeling scattered and burnt out.

Today, many of us try to make sanctuaries out of our living spaces. Here we attempt to escape from the encroaching complexity of modern life, with its electromagnetically charged computers and mobile phones.

Never before has there been a time when the pull of nature has been stronger— not just for a weekend away in the country but in our everyday lives.

Our approach to creating living spaces should be holistic, functional, and sensual, but most of all, reflect the essence of who we are. One of the ways in which we can do this is by surrounding ourselves with a "living" environment, one that takes its inspiration from the natural world. We are real people who need to live in real spaces—we are not creators of spaces for others to admire for a season or so until the next fad comes along.

Living space is sacred. It is our inner kingdom. It is a place to enjoy good food, friendship, and fun—a refuge for relaxation, contemplation, and rejuvenation, where privacy and comfort are essential.

You don't have to spend a fortune to create an environment that inspires you and tantalizes your senses. Great beauty may be found in small things. Enjoy the transitory gifts of each season by collecting treasures such as twigs, pebbles, and wild grasses, and extend that simple beauty to your home. Arrange your other personal treasures to reflect your mood.

The renewal of each season allows us to renew ourselves. Breathe new life into areas that have cocooned you through the stillness of winter, or prepare for the new life of spring

with a good cleansing. Reinvent a room in a day by changing fabrics or finding new homes for old paintings. Experiment with changing the position of your bed to alter your perspective completely.

The possibilities are endless, the palette dizzying, and the potential unlimited.

Raw need not be rustic, unfinished, or untreated. It's about layering the old with the new. Think shiny with smooth, or rough and textured. The focus is on mixing the natural with modern convenience. Raw materials are timeless, suited to all styles of decorating, and by their nature they belong in any environment.

In this book you'll find both relaxed and sophisticated ways to incorporate raw materials into building and design. With down-to-earth simplicity it's easy to create a living-friendly atmosphere—one that's timeless, functional, stylish, and affordable.

RAW

RAW

METAL

Metals do not simply serve a practical purpose. They offer reflective surfaces that may be beaten, oxidized, or left in a silvery smooth pristine state to create architectural designs and artistic expressions. Whatever effect you wish to achieve, metal has a place in decoration.

Modern designs include metal for functionality. Iron and steel fortify structures as well as beautify them. Wrought iron, galvanized metal, stainless steel, pewter, and aluminum all enhance architectural designs. Corrugated tin is affordable and practical as a roofing material suited to many climates—particularly if one enjoys the sound of rain hitting the roof during a thunderstorm.

Stainless-steel surfaces are practical in modern kitchens—and look spectacular when incorporated into the facades of buildings where they offer a cool contrast to warmer materials. Wrought iron is crafted for solid railings, staircases, or garden accessories and outdoor furniture. In recent years aluminum and pewter have been shaped into decorative cutlery, door handles, napkin rings, and frames. Increasingly important for structural purposes, too, aluminum and steel add reflective edginess to contrast with subtle and soothing opposites.

Innovative and trendy artisans now recycle scrap metals to sculpture functional artworks, expressing another side to the often mundane uses of metal. In its various forms and reflective values, metal has found an integral place in decoration and design. Always cool to the touch, metal delivers a refreshing and soothing effect on all interiors.

PREVIOUS PAGE: Industrial metal sheeting has been custom cranked to a specific radius, creating the effect of a domed ceiling. The walls have been kept white to emphasize clean architectural lines.
RIGHT: Reflective utilitarian surfaces made of cool, blue stainless steel deliver a refreshingly functional yet stylish edge to this understated modern kitchen.

LEFT AND BELOW: This metal staircase, which connects two floors, was created by two South African artists, Guy du Toit and David Rossouw. A functioning, living piece of art, it is sculpted from construction metal. Each step embodies the different elements—earth, air, fire, metal, and water—using different materials. The staircase also

features a fan, pieces of broken glass, and running water. From every angle in this house there is visual interaction with the symmetry of wood and metal.

RIGHT: In this open-plan kitchen, the silvery metallic curves of the stainless-steel door handles and industrial light fittings combine well with the earthy colors of the plastered walls and limestone floors.

LEFT: Get away from it all without leaving home in

this bedroom designed with a flushed metal ceiling.

Pale colors, wooden floors, and minimal decorating

are the ingredients of this serene, uncluttered space.

From the window you can gaze across a vast horizon and enjoy majestic sunsets.

ABOVE: A metal rail and cotton hanging shelf have been used to create this simple and

practical storage solution, which allows clothing to breathe.

PREVIOUS PAGES: In the loving hands of a master crafter, metal

may be beaten and bent into

whimsical shapes. Naively

plastered walls have been

spontaneously dotted with

colored glass and confidently

coated in vibrant hues.

ABOVE: Scour street markets for home accessories such as this

bent-wire bath rack.

RIGHT: Metal fittings and accessories blend well with wood.

ABOVE: Custom-designed wrought-iron railings and animal-design patio furniture add a whimsical flavor to outdoor spaces.

RIGHT: On the exterior of this modern home, corrugated metal has been sculpted into the integral design. Plastered walls and paving celebrate the use of raw material and create an impressive facade.

LEFT AND RIGHT:

Metal may seem an

unusual element to use

in an interior because of

its hard, steely, and often

cold appearance. Yet in most forms—as seen here with this simple

painted kitchen table with a metal top—it adds a cool contrast to

warmer finishes. In recent years, metals such as aluminum, pewter, and

stainless steel have become popular materials for everyday items that are

functional yet artistic.

RAW

RAW

WOOD

The numbing mélange of endless traffic jams and gray buildings makes most people yearn for quiet and a sense of order. We look to the trees in lush indigenous forests and fragrant pine plantations for their magnificent healing nature. We use the expression "knock on wood," which seems to imbue wood with sacred powers and protective qualities.

Wood has been used for centuries for construction, work surfaces, and art forms. Wood appeals to our senses; we intuitively touch those surfaces that capture our attention. Unusual knotty grains and textures delight the eye, while subtle aromas linger long after the tree has left the forest.

Wood shares a sympathetic symbiosis with nature by aesthetically fusing with all other raw materials.

Think eco-friendly before buying lumber. Ensure that the wood comes from sustainable sources, where it is quickly replenished. Better suppliers will have a good forestry policy and should know the properties and qualities of each wood. Whenever possible, recycle old wood.

Forests function as the lungs of the earth; they purify and cleanse the air we breathe, and add grace to our landscapes. It is essential that each of us plays our part in preserving this precious resource.

PREVIOUS PAGE: Nothing could be simpler than using scaffolding planks for wooden flooring, such as these found in a builders' yard. The design of this house allows the wood to be visible from all angles. With more people working from home these days, living spaces are being redefined by their flexibility to evolve into work spaces.
RIGHT: A single aluminum lamp offers stark contrast to an organic palette of ocher-pigmented, roughly plastered walls and aging wood. Cool concrete slabs for shelving and sleek modern surfaces tempered with earthy and weathered textures create a crucial balance.

PREVIOUS PAGES: In this idyllic country cabin, the walls, ceiling, floor, and even tables and chairs are made from different varieties of wood. The sleek lines of contemporary furniture and Zen-inspired jug and bowls offer streamlined simplicity against a rustic backdrop.

LEFT: The levels seem to soar to lofty heights in this home; the environment seems to expand endlessly. The myriad patterns, shapes, and textures of wood found here can be combined with other raw materials, in ways to suit tastes that are organic or urban chic.

ABOVE: Integration of outdoor and indoor makes this generous space seem even more generous. The symmetry of wood and its knotty appearance adds textural interest. Wind-block windows and large door openings have been designed to allow in cool breezes and an abundance of natural light.

ABOVE AND RIGHT: If it is protected, wood weathers well against natural forces. However, overexposure to sun, wind, and rain will wear wooden doors and window frames over time, eventually resulting in an appealing bleached look with characteristic cracks. To nourish and preserve raw wood, regularly apply coats of thinned linseed oil or beeswax with a soft rag.

RIGHT: In this fusion of East and West and old and new, a contemporary dining suite composed of artificial and natural materials coexists with a lustrous wooden floor and the intricate hand-carvings on the display cabinet from India. The floor has a painted trompe l'oeil carpet, appropriately breaking up a large, neutral space with a colorful, artistic alternative.

LEFT AND THIS PAGE: As we bring the elements of texture, light, form, and color into our own environment by using raw materials, we strengthen our connection to the earth. Here, a naive arrangement of twigs and branches in a glass, with carved wooden cups and bowls from North Africa and Indonesia, have been placed to reflect the mood of the moment.

LEFT: Polished teak beams with eucalyptus poles spaced intermittently between them add an informal

touch to the muted family room. Two wooden armoires balanced proportionately in the room are

complemented by knotty kilims, which cover a concrete floor, and art deco chairs.

ABOVE: A comforting space with the bare essentials: a burning candle, second-hand wooden table

with homemade shelf, and fairy-tale wrought-iron furniture.

RIGHT: Chairs made from laminated plywood are left in their original state, unmolded

and uncovered. They have been fitted with metal casters, allowing the chairs to move and

swivel freely. Inspirational in design yet functional for entertaining, this dining room may

also be transformed into an informal boardroom for impromptu meetings.

BELOW: This open-plan space is joined by a seamless, suspended catwalk that

separates the guest suite from the main bedroom and bathroom in this home.

Internal windows and skylights allow light to flood the inner sanctum.

PREVIOUS PAGES: In this urban family kitchen, naturally scented cedar-wood cabinets have been limewashed for a bleached, matte look that contrasts with the polished granite surfaces and the sleek metal stove unit. Easy-to-clean concrete floors, tinted to organic hues with powdered pigments, have been scored into symmetrical slabs and sealed with linseed oil.

LEFT: Wood appeals to all our senses. Its availability, plus the ease with which it can be transformed and shaped, has made it an ideal material for buildings objects and creating sculptural carvings.

Indulge in collecting wooden items. Whether traditionally made modern pieces or timeless treasures, structural beams or *objets d'art*, wood reflects a character and warmth that synthetic materials simply do not have.

RAW

RAW
PLASTER

Whether mixed with water and smeared onto a floor, petrified over time into stone, or baked into bricks, dirt has been the most common building material since the beginning of time.

Where regions lack lumber and stone, indigenous peoples use earth itself to build their homes. Where other materials are available, many may simply daub the framework of a hut with mud. Modern humans have refined this method with synthetic materials such as cement, concrete, and plaster, all suited to harsh climates and the demanding modern lifestyle. Adobe, raw plaster, and clay have natural insulation properties and the added pleasure of the delicate, sweet aroma of earth.

Homes made from earth-colored plaster, brick, or clay are the epitome of living in the raw. These houses usually feel cool and blend in with the natural environment. The style can be continued indoors with minimal decoration and natural fabrics and fibers. Highly durable and able to withstand normal traffic, plastered walls and floors are naturally handsome.

Plastered walls can have a deep, textural relief or a smooth, sophisticated hardness, depending on application. In most cases plaster can be tinted to a variety of shades, using powdered pigments and oxides. Plastering techniques can imitate the cool effect of stone or chalky frescoed walls, revolutionizing wall coverings and the feeling of space.

PREVIOUS PAGE: Plaster may be tinted to a variety of subtle, earthy shades using colored pigments and powdered oxides.
RIGHT: This creamy wall has been troweled to a smooth finish for a sophisticated look. The plaster was then sealed with tinted wax.

BELOW AND RIGHT: Plastered walls offer a refreshing retreat from the scorching summer sun. A friendly material to live with, raw plaster "breathes" well, allowing moisture to evaporate easily. Walls textured with plaster are best left in their chalky, natural state or washed with the slightest tint of color. Plastered walls combined with wooden floors work well for both urban chic and modern country styles.

PREVIOUS PAGES: Raw materials, as used on the exterior of this house, blend with the surrounding natural environment.

BELOW AND RIGHT: Textured, natural plaster walls have a different allure to that of the flat, synthetic surfaces of wallpaper, vinyl, and paint. It is possible to texture plaster by scoring the

wet surface with an assortment of tools. Try adding coarse sea sand to the plaster mix for a slightly rougher finish. Or you could incise a border of small stones, river pebbles, or crystals sunken in wet plaster.

In this photographic studio, hand-plastered walls combine well with a concrete floor to create a cool, earthy work space. Decorative metalwork adds the personal, transforming finishing touches.

LEFT AND BELOW: In this kitchen, finely plastered walls have been smoothed to perfection and tinted an ocher hue. The concrete screed floor has been scored into large shapes to look like paving stones.

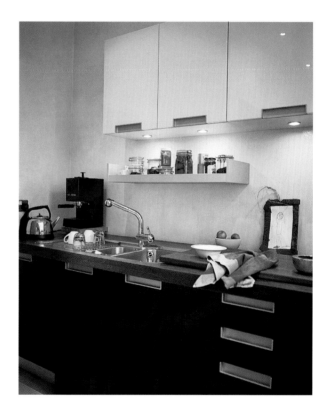

With its dark walnut unit and cool metal stove, the kitchen is fuss-free, functional, modern, and elegant.

LEFT AND ABOVE: When wet, plaster can be manipulated and transformed into any design. The amount of texture depends entirely on the look you desire. Raw plaster has a warm and ancient quality—the look is influenced by African styles. Heavily textured plaster has an undiluted rustic appeal, which can be tempered with sparse aluminum accessories.

LEFT AND RIGHT: Concrete is the modern equivalent of stone. In many aspects of contemporary architecture, it has taken the place of stone by offering a sense of weight and solidity with very little effort and cost. Left raw it has a distinctly industrial look, although its starkness can be softened with tints or paints, or in clever combination with lumber and colorful fabrics.

The industrial effect of the concrete slabs punctuating the walls of this architect's home is warmed by Zimbabwean teak floors.

LEFT AND RIGHT: Concrete is truly the defining material of modern architecture because of its affordability and minimalistic appearance.

It has given new meaning to the concept "functionality." Indoors it is most commonly found on floors, although it is also suited to shelving, built-in bed bases, benches, baths, and other furniture. In this home, chunks of scored concrete slabs have been used to create the look of flagstones.

FOLLOWING PAGES: Textural qualities can be incorporated into any good architectural design and are particularly effective when making use of the available light.

RAW

MASONRY

Stone may be introduced in the home in the smallest of ways: an arrangement of stones around the base of a tree, in a jar, or as a border of river pebbles embedded in the ground. On the other hand, you may decide on a solid stone house. Whichever style you choose, stone offers a way to celebrate the ordinary things from our amazingly abundant world.

Stone and brick may be married harmoniously with elements such as wood and metal; they support each other in an aesthetic and structural way.

The ancient media of brick and stone have always suggested antiquity and solidity. Each piece of stone is unique in shape and almost indestructible—it invariably improves with the weathering of time.

Sandstone, limestone, slate, and other stones lend themselves to both structural building work and intricate or simple paving designs—mixed with standard building bricks or quarried tiles, stone will create a stunning visual patchwork with permanence.

PREVIOUS PAGE: An old wall has been stripped to its original state, revealing solid stone.
RIGHT: In this bathroom the mix of modern white tiles and rugged gray slate is easy to maintain.

LEFT: Building bricks have been used to create the floor in this modern architect's home. An industrial grinding machine was used to smooth and level the top surface.

ABOVE: This outdoor table top is made from a thick slab of gray slate.

LEFT: Use "masonry" materials for simple decoration—

display beach pebbles and shells in bowls or baskets.

RIGHT: In this bathroom, a sensual palette of neutral

shades, sandstone tiles, and beech flooring work in

perfect synergy. In climates with hot summers, these

materials offer cool refreshment to tired and aching skin.

LEFT: This sleek, pale, maple side unit softens the effect of rough stone walls.

ABOVE AND RIGHT: Bricks are the basic building block of architectural evolution and the most common material used since the beginning of time. Used in minimal quantities, bricks add character to a room and have a warming influence; too much, however, tends to make spaces feel dark and imposing.

BELOW: This bathroom was created to provide the ultimate sensual retreat. Pale and mottled glass mosaic tiles lend purity to the shower, in sharp contrast to the slate, which is rugged with dark, variegated coloring.

BELOW: Slate is remarkably versatile: it can function as interior or exterior flooring, or as paving, roofing, or shelving material. It is available in many colors, from gold to blue, gray, charcoal, and black. Slate coordinates with any decorating scheme, such as in this minimalist bathroom, where personal accessories like candles and incense suggest quiet contemplation and rejuvenation.

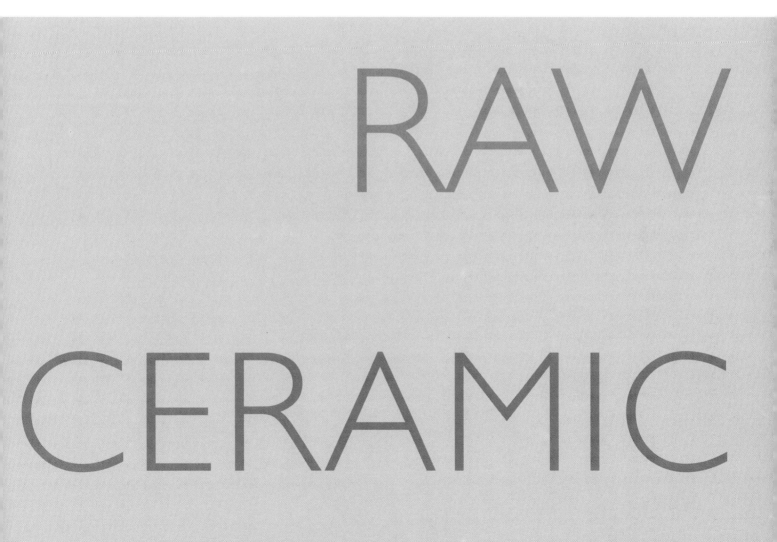

RAW

RAW
CERAMIC

Smooth and glazed or crude and rugged, ceramic materials imbue a rustic quality to surfaces and functional items. Natural, uncolored clay tiles and pots are available in many sizes and color variations, from deep, burnished browns to tawny reds and fiery golds, which add warmth to living spaces. The colors are usually influenced by the region in which the clay was found. Color may also be affected by oils rising to the surface during firing, which create an authentic patina. An occasional injection of passionately colored mosaic tiles creates a strong visual contrast to this organic palette.

Ceramists understand the behavior of the materials they use and know the best clay for each individual piece, whether it is a sculptural piece of art or a functional floor tile.

Ceramic materials are timeless, suited to all styles of decorating—try placing large clay bowls of cinnamon sticks on a festive table, or simply add a row of naively painted tiles for decoration. By its very nature, clay has a sense of belonging to the environment. In surrounding ourselves with earthen materials we are putting ourselves back in touch with the environment.

PREVIOUS PAGE: Yin and Yang ceramic bowls with chopsticks have been placed in minimal arrangement to create an informal dining setting. Simple and uncluttered, a stem of bamboo leaves stands in a wooden vase, offering a soothing splash of green.
RIGHT: Dipping bowls and plates in varying shades of celadon and sage green are multifunctional accessories that are also rewarding to the eye.

BELOW: Ceramics instantly add a sense of earthen goodness to an interior. Shapely platters and nomadic stoneware bowls make beautiful everyday items. They are at their best left in plain, earthy colors with a matte finish.

BELOW: An arrangement of stoneware bowls in various heights, sizes, and styles creates a stunning and eclectic feature of curved forms and pristine lines. Ceramics may be finely glazed or burnished, or left naive, granular, and rustic.

PREVIOUS PAGES: A ceramist's studio in the

desert overflows with works in progress.

LEFT AND ABOVE: The magnificent art of mosaic

has been practiced for centuries. Small pieces of ceramic, stone, or glass tesserae are placed

close together, embedded in wet cement in three-dimensional, whimsical designs. Mosaics can

be incorporated into any architectural design and made an integral part of the building.

BELOW AND RIGHT: Used to decorate table tops and shower floors or to surround a window or mirror frame, mosaics add a colorful artistic detail in geometric patterns or renditions of everyday scenes. They also enliven otherwise cold, stark surfaces.

This concrete screed floor and basin unit (*RIGHT*) are tinted blue and green to complement the bright mosaic tiles in the

shower, creating a pleasing visual symmetry. Roughly plastered walls add to the overall textural appeal. Mosaics look so simple, and it is certainly worth trying to create one yourself, but it does require patience and hard work. The design is fundamental and correct materials are essential. Begin with an old garden pot before trying out that floor you have in mind.

LEFT AND RIGHT:

Naive designs add a personal touch when decorating with mosaic. A hand-painted ceramic

basin found in Mexico incorporates almost every color under the sun. It is set in

concrete screed, which has been painted red. Copper laboratory piping and taps

are an innovative alternative to the standard items.

THIS PAGE AND RIGHT: Terra-cotta pots of all shapes and sizes, filled to the brim with flowers, culinary herbs, or cacti, make a simple, innovative sculptural feature when embedded into concrete or plastered walls. They offer an excellent solution for expansive stretches of exterior walls, or when growing miniature gardens. Ceramic pots and tiles may have natural color or variations on the surface, unique to every single piece; this is largely influenced by the region in which the clay is found.

PREVIOUS PAGES: This garden mosaic was created using loose pieces of marble left over from a cutting yard. Recycle marble, stone, or glass to make your own designs at home.

LEFT AND RIGHT: Small, evenly shaped, glazed green tesserae combined with a matte stone inlay are set in a refined geometric border to magnificent effect on this wrought-iron table. Weatherproof and easy to clean, a mosaic table top is the practical choice for family breakfasts outside. At last mosaics are no longer used just for decorating swimming pools. Experiment with creating homemade mosaics incorporating shells, pebbles, and crystals.

RAW

RAW

TEXTILES

Textiles are often the starting point to planning a decorating scheme. We may see a fabric with enormous appeal and begin to seek ways of using it. A vibrantly colored kilim can be thrown over a sofa, or a simple sheet of muslin can be loosely draped over a open window.

Textiles are not only a way of adding color to our interiors. They also introduce the element of texture, with their contrasting weaving techniques and innovative designs. These woven delights come in different thicknesses, textures, and styles. They add warmth and comfort to tiles, floorboards, or couches, and silky softness to bed linen.

For understated simplicity, dress cold areas with raw materials such as hemp or jute. On balmy days, keep fabrics sheer around windows to allow fresh breezes to diffuse through finely woven yarns.

For centuries, different cultures have woven mystical and magical legends into their textiles. Traditionally, people conveyed messages about their heritage, their family, their region, or their religious faith, all through the patterns and colors they chose as they wove. In some cultures, woven textiles have great value and may represent a family's wealth.

Different patterns and textures lend themselves to different seasons throughout the year. In summer, stick to cool cotton. Keep the silk, cashmere, and velvet for cooler weather.

PREVIOUS PAGE: Textured white waffle-weave cotton gown, socks, and a blanket-stitched throw are inviting in cooler weather.
RIGHT: Vibrant cloths from North Africa are displayed here to their best advantage against a stone wall, which acts as a neutral backdrop to offset the exquisite hand-woven textiles.

LEFT: This four-poster bed has been draped with crisp, white organdy cotton, which has a simple ladder stitch running through it at intervals. It is a perfect example of how to create privacy while maintaining the view.

TOP RIGHT: Lightweight and cool—nothing competes with the comfort of crisp cotton.

CENTER RIGHT: Embroidered designs and patterns on cotton and linen offer an unobtrusive textured effect.

BELOW RIGHT: Sheer slip-covers in white make an elegant dressing for occasional chairs.

BELOW: Pale-colored stitching in this cotton cushion cover,

with an olive wicker chair, works for an organic palette. The

look is soft and subdued, and completely natural.

RIGHT: A basket-weave woven cotton has been used to cover

this contemporary styled sofa. Ecru- and chocolate-colored

raffia cushions are piled invitingly on top.

BELOW: Pamper yourself with textural pleasures that are heaven to touch. Try cashmere or velvet for the epitome of sensual luxury. This Zen-inspired bedroom setting is created with a Japanese futon, tatami mats, and an artful layering of vibrant colors and textures on Yoruba cloth, red chenille cushions, and a cherry-colored throw.

RIGHT: Textural interest in this living room appears boldly in the form of ruby-colored Egyptian Bedouin rugs and a sofa in burgundy-colored corduroy.

A wooden day-bed is an interesting and natural alternative to a sofa, which complements the wooden trestle table and floor. This setting reflects a proportioned balance of contemporary and traditional elements.

LEFT: Piles of fringed woolen textiles, waffle-weave hand towels, Hampton linen, and blanket-stitched throws make wonderful home accessories. They may be shifted around to suit changing moods, seasons, and trends.

Throw fabric over a bed and instantly change the ambience in a room, or add chunky weaves for textural impact. Introduce luxurious wool or linen weaves to sofas, pillows, and beds for snuggling up in cooler weather.

RIGHT: Fabric may be stretched over panels or frames and displayed in a way that decoratively fills a vast space. Combinations of natural and artificial materials complement each other in soothing shades of pink and green, inspired by nature. The stark, stainless-steel detail on the chairs is a welcome contrast to the rich, warm hues of the wooden flooring.

LEFT: A perfect nest for lazy summer days has been created with these beautifully woven textiles found in locations all over Africa. Casually placed upon a wooden daybed and grass mat, the silk throw and cushion covers complete a comfortable and relaxed afternoon setting.

ABOVE: A healthy environment in which to live: natural sisal flooring and pure cotton sheets are kind to our bodies and pleasing to the touch.

ABOVE AND RIGHT: A kilim from Afghanistan adds bold visual contrast to earthy, plastered walls and a sandstone floor. Functional and beautiful, this piece is displayed to its full splendor when it is used as a curtain and drawn closed.

LEFT AND RIGHT: Intricate patterns draw the eye, and complex arrangements tempt us to look again, to feel, and sometimes to gaze with wonder at the design. Use textiles to highlight a display of personal treasures, or layers of soft fabrics to create spaces that radiate serenity and comfort.

RAW

FIBER

Natural fibers such as sisal, coir, sea grass, raffia, jute, hemp, and banana leaves are all hardy, easy-to-care-for coverings ideal for a warm climate. They are available in a myriad savanna-tinted hues.

Sisal is a tough, long-lasting fiber traditionally used in Kenya for roofing and making baskets. Sisal and coir share a distinctive coarseness which, when used for floor matting, is therapeutic for bare feet. Jute is a soft, silky fiber—as it is not particularly resilient, it is often mixed with other natural fibers to add strength. Jute can be found in anything from wrapping paper to cloth.

Burlap is also a coarse fabric, usually made from a blend of jute and hemp. A rough and versatile fiber, hemp is now in demand by consumers for its durability and texture. Ideal for floor rugs, throws, and unusual window coverings, it creates a rugged, rustic look that celebrates the natural environment.

Other useful and beautiful fibers are the illala palm, bamboo, and the grasses grown for thatching and basketry. They can all be sculpted and woven into sofas, chairs, and screens. They are naturally water repellent, cool in summer, and warm in winter.

These fibers come from renewable resources, making them important in a sustainable environmental system—they are the ultimate eco-friendly option when it comes to surfaces that need to put up with a rigorous lifestyle. Commercial support of traditionally made woven crafts ensures that this ancient skill and knowledge will always remain part of our global heritage.

PREVIOUS PAGE: Simple sea-grass matting enhances this informal Zen-style dinner setting.
RIGHT: Casual fiber floor coverings like this sisal rug add texture, which is offset in this room by the smooth lines of the lavishly upholstered leather sofa.

BELOW: Grass matting, banana leaves, sisal, and raffia are excellent natural fabrics for everyday items such as coasters, exfoliating loofahs, bags, and lampshades. The natural coarseness of raw-fiber slippers provide a gentle massage.

BELOW: Scour the markets in your home area or vacation destination for favorite ethnic crafts, and use them for storage or display. A collection of handwoven baskets will add symmetry to a sparsely decorated room.

LEFT: Serene whites and organic sandstone add up to a peaceful bathroom. Grass matting infuses the cool, pale interior with warm, earthy tones. Light, space, and raw

materials are like a soothing tonic at the end of an energetic day.

ABOVE: A cinder-block supported table and a hemp rug create a laid-back, nomadic look.

BELOW: The careful selection of clean lines and raw-fiber floor coverings (sisal and coir) in this living

area coordinates simplicity with luxury.

RIGHT: The bamboo window screen, ladder, and side table in this bedroom live in happy fusion with

the rich yet soft tones of the wooden headboard (made from an African Tonga door). The embroidered

throws and silk cushions soften the impact, allowing all the elements to combine comfortably,

BELOW: Use wicker baskets to store or display personal items.

RIGHT: Sisal, shown here, is a tough and lasting fiber from the *Agava sisalana*, a cactus-like plant that grows naturally in tropical climates. Suitable for whole rooms or as matting and runners, it is available in a fine or heavy bouclé in varied designs and colors.

Sisal, coir, jute, and hemp are natural choices when decorating with raw wood and hand-plastered walls.

LEFT: Sea grass is another versatile fiber—and it has nothing to do with the sea; in fact, it is cultivated inland.

Sea grass, along with other natural fibers, is finding its way into every accessory and onto most domestic surfaces. These days, for example, there are sisal-covered ice buckets, woven grass mats, baskets and coasters, raffia handbags, and wicker serving trays.

These products celebrate traditional weaving methods, which are a large part of our global heritage. And when it comes to aesthetic appeal, they have no competition from their artificial counterparts.

LEFT AND RIGHT: Bamboo, the great towering fibrous grass, is not to be underestimated. Flexible, lightweight, and resilient, it has been used for centuries as a building material. Bamboo poles make good fencing as well as false roofing to conceal unsightly ceilings. When bamboo is split it may also be made into garden gates and wall panels and woven into hats, mats, or baskets. It is even made into food—in many countries bamboo shoots are an exotic treat. Bamboo propagates easily with a good supply of water, and is often seen growing on steep hillsides to prevent soil erosion.

LEFT AND RIGHT:

Modern design is plain

and minimal. It has been

achieved successfully in

this living area through the choice of contemporary furniture pieces made

from natural materials. The clean lines are offset by the rough textural quality

of the wicker chair and sisal floor covering. Simple and uncluttered, this

interior exudes peace.

LEFT AND RIGHT: Woven baskets and bowls make decorative storage containers—with their different weaves and designs they add strong textural elements to an interior. These traditional grass mats from Japan and North Africa complete simple table settings.

The popularity of natural fibers prevents traditional knowledge from being eroded by the proliferation of artificial alternatives.

Wood and building supplies

Ace Hardware
2200 Kensington Ct.
Oak Brook , IL 60523
Tel: (630990-6600
www.acehardware.com

Home Depot
2455 Pace Ferry Rd.
Atlanta, GA 30339
Tel: (800)430-3376
www.homedepot.com

Lowe's Home Improvement
Warehouse
P.O. Box 1111
North Wilkesboro, NC 28656
Tel: (800)44-LOWES
www.lowes.com

Modern Wood Works
www.modernwoodworks.com

True Value
8600 Bryn Mawr
Chicago, IL 60631
Tel: (877)474-9054
www.truevalue.com

Villager's Hardware
1 Crag Rd.
South Plainfield, NJ 07080
Tel: (908)222-9400
www.homedepot.com

Mosaic and tile

Charles Tiles, Inc.
760 County Rt. 523
Stockton, NJ 08559
Tel: (609)379-0330
Fax: (609)397-1277
www.charlestiles.com

Import Gallery
www.importgallery.com

Mosaic Mercantile, Inc.
461 end St. #331
San Francisco, CA 94107
Tel: (877)9-MOSAIC
www.mosaicmerc.com

Mosaic Supply
10427 1/2 Unit A Rush St.
S. El Monte, CA 91733
Tel: (626)279-7020
www.mosaicsupply.com

Nemo Tile Company, Inc.
48 East 21st St.
New York, NY 10010
Tel: (212)505-0009
www.nemotile.com

Painted Earth
Tel: (877)505-TILE
Fax: (512)381-4574
www.paintedearth.com

Piece by Piece Mosaics
Tel: (203)256-0644
Fax: (203)256-5843
www.piecebypiece.com

Universe of Mosaic Art
www.UMAmosaics.com

US Tile
909 W. Railroad St.
Corona, CA 92882
Tel: (909)737-0200
Fax: (909)734-9591
www.ustile.com

Marble and stone

Buckingham-Virginia Slate
Corporation
1 Main St./P.O. Box 8
Arvonia, VA 23004
Tel: (804)581-1131
Fax: (804)581-1130
www.bvslate.com

Buddy Rhodes Studio, Inc.
2130 Oakdale Ave.
San Francisco, CA 94124
Tel: (877)706-5303
www.BuddyRhodes.com

Custom Marble Design
7311 Grove Rd. Ste. N
Fredericck, MD 21704
Tel: (800)861-6707
Fax: (301)695-6584
www.fwp.net/CutomMarbleDesign/

Null Original Designs
40 4th St.
Petaluma, CA 94952
Tel: (800)722-NULL
www.nulldesigns.com

Vermont Structural Slate Company
Box 98
3 Prospect St.
Fair Haven, VT 05743
Tel: (800)343-1900
Fax: (802)265-3865
www.vermontstructuralslate.com

Pewter and wrought iron

Argento Designs
8570 Casanova Rd.
Atascadero, CA 93422
Tel: (805)461-3000
Fax: (805)461-3000
www.aregentodesigns.com

Danforth Pewterers
P.O. Box 828
Middlebury, VT 05753
Tel: (877)DANFORTH
Fax: (802)388-0099
www.danforthpewter.com

Iron Accents
3661 Davis Bridge Rd.
Gainesville, GA 30506
Fax: (770)539-9091
www.ironaccents.com

Iron Elegance
810 Liberty St.
Painesville, OH 44077
Tel: (440)354-8386
Fax: (440)354-8389
www.ironelegance.com

Iron Source
458 Satinwood Way
Chula Vista, CA 91911
Tel: (800)869-9224
www.ironsource.com

Village Wrought Iron
7756 Main St.
Fabius, NY 13063
Tel: (315)683-5589
Fax: (315)683-5598
www.villageblacksmith.com

Wrought Iron Originals
514 Hampshire
Quincy, IL 62301
Tel: (217)221-1204
Fax: (217)221-1205
Wroughtiron.micronpcweb.com

Textile and fabric

Fabric Direct
P.O. Box 1944
Mount Marion, NY 12456
www.fabricdirect.com

Fabric Gallery
P.O. Box 540961
Merritt Island, FL 32954
www.Fabricgallery.com

Fabric Place
300 Quaker Lane
Warwick, RI 02886
Tel: (800)556-3700
www.fabricplace.com

Hancock Fabrics
3406 West Main St.
Tupelo, MS 38801
Tel: (662)844-7368
www.hancockfabrics.com

Jo-Ann Stores
5555 Darrow Rd.
Hudson, OH 44236
Tel: (800)525-4951
www.joann.com

Plaster and cement

Classic Mouldings, Inc.
226 Toryork Dr.
Toronto, Ontario
Canada M9L 1Y1
Tel: (416)745-5560
Fax: (416)745-5566
www.classicmouldings.com

General Shale Brick
P.O. Box 3547
Johnson City, TN 37602
Tel: (800)414-4661
www.generalshale.com

The Masonry Center, Inc.
1424 N. Orchard St.
P.O. Box 7825
Boise, ID 83707
Tel: (208)375-1362
Fax: (208)327-1600
www.masonrycenter.com

Young Block Company
Tel: (520)887-1234
www.youngblock.com

Metal and stainless steel

Custom-Bilt Metals
9845 Joe Vargas Way
South El Monte, CA 91733
Tel: (800)826-7813
Fax: (626)454-4785
www.custombiltmetals.com

John Boos & Company
315 South First St.
P. O. Box 609
Effingham, IL 62401
Tel: (217)347-7701
Fax: (217)347-7705
www.butcherblock.com

Lambertson Industries Inc.
490 South Rock Blvd.
Reno, NV 89502
Tel: (800)548-3324
www.lambertson.com

Sisa, coir, jute

Rugs USA.com Inc.
902 Broadway
New York, NY 10010
Tel: (800)982-7210
www.rugsusa.com

Natures Floor
Tel: (866)676-6777
www.naturesfloor.com

Rugs Rugs Rugs
Tel: (812)476-2616
www.rugsrugsrugs.com

William F. Kempf & Son
1505 Chester Pike, No. 4
Folcroft, PA 19032
Tel: (610)532-2000
Fax: (610)534-3777
www.coirmats.com

Paint

Painting Manhattan
Tel: (800)572-2126
www.paintingmanhattan.com

Artcity.com
(866)artcity
1350 Kelton Ave., Ste.308
Los Angeles, CA 90024
www.artcity.com

MisterArt.com
(800)423-7382
1800 Peachtree St. NW, Ste. 250
Atlanta, GA 30309
www.misterart.com

Art Supply Warehouse
(800)995-6778
5325 Departure Dr.
Raleigh, NC 27616
www.aswexpress.com

Ceramics, pottery and tableware

Interceramic
www.interceramicusa.com

Mary Law Pottery
1451 5th St.
Berkeley, CA 94710
Tel: (510)524-7546
www.slachmc.rice.edu/marylaw/
marylawpottery.html

Pier 1 Imports
800-245-4595
www.pier1.com

People's Pottery Inc.
One Townline Cr.
Rochester, NY 14623
Tel: (716)272-1600
Fax: (716)272-8825
www.peoplespottery.com

Pottery Barn
800-922-9934
www.potterybarn.com

Restoration Hardware
15 Koch Rd. Ste. J
Corte Madera, CA 94925
877-747-4671
www.restorationhardware.com

Rowe Pottery Works
217 West Main St.
Cambridge, WI 53523
Tel: (608)423-3935
Fax: (608)423-9826

Furniture

David Fay Custom Furniture
4115 Webster St.
Oakland, CA 94609
www.davidfay.com

Design Within Reach
455 Jackson St.
San Francisco, CA 94111
Tel: (415)837-3940
Fax: (415)835-9970
www.dwr.com

Expo Design Center
1201 Hammond Dr.
Atlanta, GA 30346
Tel: (770)913-0111

Full Upright Position
1101 N.W. Glisan
Portland, OR 97209
Tel: (800)432-5234
Fax: (503)228-6213
www.fup.com

Herman Miller for the Home
2855 44th St.
Grandville, MI 49418
Tel: (800)646-4400
Fax: (616)654-5817
www.hermanmiller.com

MoMA Design Store
44 West 53rd St.
New York, NY 10019
Tel: (800)447-6662
Fax: (610)431-3333
www.momastore.org

O Group
152 Franklin Street
New York, NY 10013
Tel: (212)431-5973
Fax: (212)431-0259
www.theorangechicken.com